T0114876

What Divorce Does

MACKEY GASKIN

WESTBOW
PRESS®
A DIVISION OF THOMAS NELSON
& ZONDERVAN

WestBow Press books may be ordered through booksellers or by contacting:

WestBow Press
A Division of Thomas Nelson & Zondervan
1663 Liberty Drive
Bloomington, IN 47403
www.westbowpress.com
844-714-3454

ISBN: 978-1-6642-0259-7 (sc)
ISBN: 978-1-6642-0258-0 (e)

Library of Congress Control Number: 2020915879

Print information available on the last page.

WestBow Press rev. date: 10/09/2020

Intro

It is becoming more rare by the year for a child to grow up in a 2 parent home. In the United States, there is one divorce approximately every 36 seconds. That's about 2,400 divorces per day. 16,800 divorces weekly. 876,000 every year. No family in our country is immune from the effects of divorce. Divorce separates children from their parents, parents from their family, and families from income. Sadly, few resources exist to help our nation's families to recover from such a devastating event. The contents of this book have helped me to understand marriage properly as it is meant to be understood and cherished. My hope is to share what my parents and I learned as a result of divorce to better help many respond to the challenges that always accompany it. This book is not only for those who have seen their marriage end in divorce. It's also for the children of divorced marriages, the friends of those who have been divorced, and for those who are afraid of getting married due to the risk of divorce.

Many millennials believe that the best way to prevent divorce is to simply move-in with their significant other and skip the whole marriage process. Sadly, this option prevents neither the emotional heartache or physical separation that comes from a painful separation. According to the Atlantic Journal statistics show that living together prior to marriage can increase the chance of getting divorced by as much as 40 percent. If living together prior to marriage does not prevent divorce, then it will not prevent a separation either. In marriage couples commit to love one another for as long as they both shall live in spite of the failings of their partner. But when a couple simply moves in together without a marital commitment, they will more than likely break-up when one finds the other to be less desirable when their personal failing presents itself.

Rest assured, there is immense hope for those who desire to be married, for those who are married, and for those who have already endured a divorce. It is my goal to help divorced parents understand how to care for and love their children, to teach readers how to care for their friends who have recently divorced, and to teach the children of divorced parents how to wisely think about their mothers and fathers.

CHAPTER 1

Children of Divorce

I have known many adults to endure a divorce, and with enough time, they have been able to move on and become healthy and whole members of society again. However, the children of divorce are not in a position to adapt in the same way as an adult. They unfortunately cannot move on by finding a new person to date or marry. In fact, just the opposite is true. The influence of their parents' divorce will most likely have a negative impact on their future romantic relationships as they may struggle to commit to and trust others later in life. How can they trust someone to never leave them for the rest of their lives if their own parents could not? Divorce splits up parents, siblings, and homes. Why would the children of divorce ever want to risk going through something like that again or worse; why would they risk putting their future children through it?

Children of divorce carry the scars of a broken family around for the rest of their lives. My wife and I will never be able to experience Christmas or Thanksgiving with both of our parents together again. Despite this reality, a parent who is aware of such things can prove to be a tremendous aid to the child. Whenever parents separate, that child now has to make a whole multitude of adult-sized choices for which he or she is not prepared. The hope for a care-free childhood is gone, and the child begins to weigh emotional decisions such as where will they spend their time and who they should go up to after games and school events? All of this may be in addition to the physical concerns of the child, such as where he or she will keep toys, clothes, and games. These are choices that no child is equipped to make, and yet millions must make them every year in the United States. Parents can help by encouraging their children to spend time with both parents, provided that each parent can provide a physically and emotionally safe environment for their children.

My parents divorced when I was two years old, so I have no memory of our little family. I do not remember ever playing with them at the same time or reading to me. I do not even remember them sitting together. As a result, I experienced real stress after every one of my baseball games, recognition ceremonies, and any other event where they were both present because I had no idea who I should go to after the event. As early as the age of five, I was aware that I would upset one of my parents no matter who I went to first. I was left with that decision, and I was never prepared for it. This type of social anxiety is hard for adults to navigate, let alone small children, yet children of divorced parents have to experience decisions like these regularly. It does not matter if they are only 5 years old or 25 years old--it is still an agonizing choice.

I recommend following the wisdom of my own mother, who advocated for the other parent--even at her own expense. When I was young she told me to go to my father first. She knew I loved her, and she chose not to be hurt by it. Divorced parents, please allow your children the freedom to choose the other, and make sure they know that you will not be hurt.

In most cases, divorce is not going to be better for children. Having two homes, two Christmases, and two rooms will never compare to having a whole family all living under one roof. They will have to learn how to live in two cultures: that of their mother's house and that of their father's house. No two people are exactly alike, and it is inevitable that the parents will manage their households differently. These cultures may be similar, but to ask a child to learn two cultures is to ask them to never be truly comfortable in one or the other. So, be very sensitive to how your children are feeling. Ask them questions, and make sure they know they can tell you anything, and that you won't be hurt by it (or that you will not express your hurt). This will pay major dividends as the children grow. They will be much more likely to share about the struggles they are having that inevitably come with adolescence, and they will have a secure relationship with their parents, which will allow them to gain valuable wisdom.

Now, perhaps the hardest thing you will do as a parent is to give your children the right to choose to not spend time with you and to instead spend time with the other parent. Andrew Peterson, a musician, sings a song about marriage called "Dancing in the Minefield," and any married individual can speak to the truth that even the smallest of issues can start a fight. This minefield is all the more present in a divorce, it almost always begins with an emotional landmine. Despite the history that exists with the other parent, it is important to respect them as the parent of your children, and your children desperately need a healthy relationship with both of you. Encouraging a child to spend time with the other parent does not mean that he or she is merely kicked out on the weekends. Instead, work to make sure your home is a warm and welcoming place, and whenever they want to go see the other parent, do not show any sadness or anger. This also means that it is inappropriate to speak hatefully of the other parent. Lastly, it is very tempting to have your child communicate on behalf of one parent to the other, especially if they are going to be seeing them anyway few things could be more harmful or destructive for your child.

Resist the temptation to use your child as a shield so that you can avoid having to have a challenging conversation with the other parent. Children look to their parents to be their protectors, and it should never be the other way around. Communication, even if about minute details, should not be managed by the child. Current technology makes communication even easier than in the past. It seems like every digital platform has a chat feature, even if it's a simple text message or email. The children of divorce however, are not a chat feature. that is a burden they should never have to carry.

Something else that also must be considered upon a divorce is that the children may not feel very comfortable in a new home or in the same home that is missing one of their parents. Thankfully, there are some things you can try to alleviate your child's stress. Offer to play their favorite games with them, watch their favorite shows with them, or read their favorite stories with them. Doing something intentionally that they enjoy will go a long way toward helping them begin to feel comfortable again. However, be mindful that you do not try to dictate what emotions your children should be feeling. When a person is truly comfortable, he or she will let their guard down and say what he or she really thinks and feels. Therefore, let your children know that you want to hear how they are feeling, whether it's good or bad. Let them know that they can complain and vent to you and that you will not get mad at them but that you intend to listen to them. Simply being a good listener can often relieve the tension, stress, and emotions that children are dealing with. Other times, they may need your help on how to best understand and view the abrupt life change they are experiencing as a result of the divorce.

Slow Movie Zombies

Have you ever watched a zombie television show or movie? Often, the zombies are slow-walking, annoying creatures bent on human destruction that look easy enough to escape. The problem is when the characters are surrounded by hundreds of zombies that overwhelm them. Thankfully, as a child I never encountered zombies, but I did experience some consistent annoyances from my parents' divorce. One of them was the challenge of always making sure my clothes and belongings were always where they needed to be. If I wanted to wear a specific shirt, or if I needed to have the correct clothes for baseball or basketball, I had to think ahead about which parent I would be staying with that weeknight and what I would need for the following day. That may not seem like much, but very few of my friends had to deal with this struggle. They just went home to the same house each day that had everything that they needed whenever they needed it. I often felt surrounded and anxious about a lot of small decisions that I alone had to make everyday.

So how do you help your child handle the annoyance of going back and forth and having everything that they need? 1) Get ready for forgetfulness: Learning to plan days in advance is a great skill for children to learn, but it won't come without some bumps along the way. When they remember late at night that they need specific clothing for the next day, be willing to drive them over to the other parent's that night or the next morning before school so that they can have the peace of mind of being prepared for the day ahead. Do not punish them for having to navigate two homes by allowing them to be humiliated for not having what they need at school or practice. They did not cause their life to be split between two homes, and it is no surprise when they struggle to adjust to this new normalcy. 2) Do not pressure your children to bring more of their belongings to your house. Newsflash: They may not be comfortable in your home without the other parent. This does not mean that they dislike you, but often children bond more with one parent than the other at different seasons of their life, and they may prefer to leave the majority of their clothing and belongings where they feel most comfortable at that time. However, do be sure to provide a place for them to keep their clothes, toys, and school supplies, because there may come a time when they do feel more comfortable with you and will want to move more of their life under your roof, both literally and figuratively.

Time away from home

One of my favorite things to do when I was a child was to have my friends over to spend the night or to go over to their house for the night. Most children enjoy a sleepover, especially children who have recently experienced a divorce. It may be nice for them to get away and spend time with a family who are all under one roof. However, this fun event may be on one of the few nights a week that they are scheduled to stay with you. There is no doubt that children need to spend time with both their father and mother. But they also need friends their own age to develop their social and relational skills. Every now and again, be willing to sacrifice some time with the children so that they can spend time with trusted friends who serve as a good influence. This means being willing to pick them up from their other parent's house only to drop them off at a friend's house. Do not limit your children's time with their friends because you think it belongs to you in the form of a custody agreement. You certainly do have the right to plan time to spend with them one-on-one, and you most definitely should, but be willing to occasionally allow your children to attend a sleepover or perhaps have a friend over.

CHAPTER 2

⋯⋯⋯⋯⋯✦⋯⋯✦⋯⋯⋯⋯⋯

How to Avoid Divorce

No one wakes up on their wedding day hoping to divorce his or her spouse. Few say, "I do" to the person that they're planning to divorce. It is never a premeditated action, and yet it happens to so many after marriage, so much so that many single people today are afraid to get married for fear of getting a divorce. They look at divorce the same way many look at cancer: with fear of being diagnosed with it. Yet, divorce is not a sudden and inevitable cancer that is beyond control. It can be avoided, and marriages can be saved, preserved, and thrive through thoughtful dating and wise decision-making.

So, how is a person to date wisely? First and foremost, wise dating requires time! Joy does not come only from having a boyfriend or girlfriend, so do not be desperate to date. Instead focus on caring for your friends well while regularly being accommodating and inviting to those you don't know yet. Our society often tells us to keep an eye out for Mr./Ms. Right, but if all we're doing is looking for someone to make us happy, will we ever become the type of person who can bring care and comfort into the lives of others? The answer is no. So, instead of trying to find the right person focus on becoming the right type of person for someone else by loving your friends well and being welcoming to those who might not have many friends yet.

As you pursue caring for others, you'll discover the gratitude and enjoyment that comes from serving others, and you'll be drawn to others who are striving to be selfless as well. You won't want to date someone who is more of a taker than a giver who is only going to take you away from your family and friends for their own desires. This mentality in dating will serve you well in discerning with whom you should pursue a romantic relationship as well as who would be a better blessing to you as simply a friend with no romantic endeavors.

It is always better to date someone who encourages you to be a more kind and considerate person. The best way to discern the effect that a relationship is having on you is to ask your friends how you have changed as a result of it. Give your friends permission to be completely honest and take their words seriously, because if they are your friends, they will be looking out for you even if they say something that is difficult to hear.

Now, I realize that many of you have already said, "I do," and you're now locked in a marriage that you may not be enjoying as much as you think you should. There is hope for you and your spouse, I promise! Your spouse never actually had the ability to make you happy. For years, movies, books, and television have taught us that we each have a certain someone who is out there for us who will complete us. Unfortunately, this is not true. It's not even close to being accurate. If it were we wouldn't see 40% of first-time marriages ending in divorce. (If you want to know who actually can complete you, skip to chapter 8. Go ahead. I'll be here when you get back.)

As a result of this long-term feeling of unhappiness and disappointment, many husbands and wives have begun looking to others to find that emotional support that they once enjoyed with their spouse. Perhaps lunch with a friend from work who laughs at their jokes and has similar interests as them or catching up with a friend from college or high school over text messaging or Facebook will meet that need. In time, what develops is an emotional and/or physical relationship with someone who is not their spouse, and they begin to resent their spouse for not treating them the way their new friend does. While this new friend may bring new happiness and energy into your life, so many people forget that in pursuing this new person they are breaking the biggest promise of their life: To love one another for better or for worse till death do you part.

Many unhappy spouses may not turn to someone they know to help fulfill the relational void in their life but instead choose to turn to someone they've never met on the internet via pornography. Statistics show that 40 million Americans regularly visit pornographic websites on webroot.com, and at least one-third of those viewers are women. Viewing pornography creates an unrealistic expectation of what love and sex actually are and will only lead to disappointment, confusion, and estrangement from your spouse. Porn is an attempt to solve a short-term problem that will only lead to long-term damage and confusion. Instead of looking to a spouse to help fulfill sexual desire and growth in intimacy, many forsake their spouse for another without ever having to leave the comfort of their home.

Instead of looking to others to fill a void in your life, look to your spouse and honestly communicate all the ways that they have hurt you and forgotten you. When we are dating, we are so focused on getting that special someone to like us that we will do backflips to gain attention and praise from them. Yet, after we marry, our hearts often seek new interests. Perhaps those interests are a career, wealth, or even another person, and our spouse is left in the emotional dust of life. So, put away your laptop, and go sit next to the lap of your husband or wife and tell them how you truly feel about them, the good and the bad. Vulnerability always leads to growth in a relationship. Don't worry about what your spouse will say, because you have no clue how they will react. Give your spouse a chance, because if the roles were reversed, would you not want someone to give you one more chance even if you had failed in the past?

I love my wife very much, and I greatly enjoy spending time with her, but she cannot bring me fulfillment or joy. My wife, like myself and all other members of humanity, is an imperfect person. Thus, as an imperfect person she cannot cause me to love her by making my life perfect. Neither can I make my wife's life perfect or complete, because I am also an imperfect person. Sure, we are both capable of making several good decisions in a day, and on those days we can make each other feel like we're on cloud 9. But, give it some time and we will oversleep, get impatient, speak harshly with one another, and be inconsiderate of one another. Neither one of us like this part of reality, but to ignore it would severely hurt our marriage. Many marriages fail because husbands and wives do not rightly consider that their spouse cannot give them the happily-ever-after about which they have always dreamed.

In addition to having some honest conversation, it is good to set up some good safeguards in your life. Minister Billy Graham made a vow to never have a one-on-one meal with any woman other than his wife. Current Vice President of the United States Mike Pence has also made a similar commitment. Those commitments may seem old and outdated, but in the 2017 "Me Too" outing of top executives, television hosts, and many others in authority who have had affairs and sexually assaulted women, two men who have not are Billy Graham and Mike Pence. It is not that these men have superior morality than others. In fact, it's just the opposite. Billy Graham has confessed to feeling like "the worst of sinners" in his sermons. It was to prevent his sin from hurting others and causing great pain that he setup a safeguard in his life. He strategically kept himself from cheating on his wife and taking advantage of his position and authority.

If you've ever vacationed in the mountains, you know that it can be a wonderful experience to be out in the mountain air, see snow-capped peaks, and look out over the vast expanse of creation from the top. However, those experiences do not come without the stress of driving up to a mountain cabin. It's full of twists and turns, with a few turns that are so sharp, you may actually see your own tail lights. On that journey, you become immensely thankful when there is a guardrail to keep you and your car on the road should you lose control of your vehicle. We need safeguards in our marriage as well. My wife and I have committed to never having a one-on-one meal with a non-relative member of the opposite gender. It's not that we don't trust ourselves or each other, but instead of putting ourselves in a position where it may appear that we are unfaithful to one another, we want just the opposite. We have decided to put up guardrails for how we spend our time and with whom we spend it.

I want your life to be a wonderful journey filled with joy. If you and your spouse choose to love one another with wise guardrails and honest communication about what you are experiencing physically and emotionally, you will experience a level of warmth and comfort with your spouse that you never knew was possible. Also, be sure to spend time with other couples. Husbands, spend time around other married men—especially older married men, and ask them what they have done to have marriages that not only last but that thrive. Wives, the same advice can be applied to you. Spend time around older wives and ask them how they have maintained and cared for their marriage well. If we only seek out those who are similar in age to us for advice we will only receive bad advice because experience is the best teacher. So go to those who have had long faithful marriages and learn from them.

Finally, for those of you who are currently married: simply don't view divorce as an option. Remember the vows you made on your wedding day. "Till death do we part... in sickness and in health... for richer or for poorer... for better or for worse." Marriage was never meant to be entered into with divorce as a viable option. Our fulfillment cannot come from another imperfect person, which is why 40% of first-time marriages end in divorce, why 70% of second-time marriages, and 90% of third-time marriages end in divorce. Another person cannot fulfill you... The grass is not greener on the other side. Therefore, when you find yourself at odds with your spouse, I encourage you to both commit to solving your conflict by any means necessary. Keep forgiving one another, keep giving one another a second chance... and hang in there... The remaining chapters will unpack the horrors of divorce, and I don't want any of you to experience them needlessly.

CHAPTER 3

Friends who are Divorced

There are some families out there who have been blessed to never have to deal with the awful consequences of divorce in their family, but we all know someone who has been divorced. There is an awkward uneasiness when we learn of a friend getting a divorce. Whether the divorce has already occurred or is in process, we can often feel small and helpless because we cannot put their marriage back together on our own. It's like driving past a car accident. You might as well just drive on, right?

Wrong.

Divorced people are lonely people, even if they're in a crowd. When the person who promised to spend the rest of their life with you leaves you—it is unbearable. The person you should have been able to trust above all others has let you down. In such a case, good friends are needed. Even if your friend is the one who caused the divorce by having an affair, they still need friendship. We all need friends to have a healthy life. So, if you know someone who has recently experienced a divorce, reach out to them. Offer to grab lunch, dinner, coffee, or simply go visit them, and if they're willing to talk about their divorce, just listen and remind them that they're not alone.

A close friend of mine from high school experienced a divorce shortly after his first year of marriage. It was a complete shock to me. They had been high school sweethearts, and many thought they would spend their whole lives together. Soon after the honeymoon, their marriage began to crumble. When I found this out I went to his house and spent a day with him just to remind him that he was not alone and that the pain and agony that he was feeling from the love of his life no longer being in his life would one day pass. Months later, he thanked me for spending time with him and he expressed how few people chose to do that. I doubt that his experience is the exception. That's why I included this chapter.

When someone you know is going through a divorce, do your best to invite them to spend time in community to show them that they are not alone. Feel free to ask them how they are feeling and what emotions and thoughts they are experiencing but do not press them to share more than they feel comfortable sharing. Remember, that the person who they should have been able to count on more than all others is no longer by their side, so they may not be ready to trust you or anyone else with such sensitive information. Therefore, it is integral that you reassure them that you want to be their friend and that you are there for them whether or not they ever feel comfortable opening up to you. Often, people want to hear the juicy news behind a divorce instead of caring for the individuals who have experienced such tremendous heartbreak.

You don't need a degree in counseling to be a good friend. You just need to be a patient and present listener. The best friends that I have in my life are the ones who will ask me personal questions about my life and my struggles. Our conversations are not always easy or pleasant, but I always walk away knowing more about myself and my problems and therefore I am able to make wiser decisions with my future. Be that type of friend to those in your life, especially to those who have experienced a divorce.

CHAPTER 4

—————————✦—————————

But I'm already Divorced

Perhaps you've been divorced for many years before you picked up this book or maybe your divorce was very recent. Either way, I want you to know that there is hope for you and your life going forward, especially if you are a parent. Divorce is never a good thing for children, but you can still make some wise decisions to care well for your children and their future. You can still have a great marriage in your future. Your children still love you in spite of what they may have already said to you. Most importantly, I want you to know that your children still *need* you. You are either their only mother or father and since it takes a mother and a father to make a child, it stands to reason that it takes a mother and a father to raise a child—even if they are divorced. So, take a deep breath in and out and dive-in with me on how to handle post-divorce life.

Divorced with Children

Your children have most likely cried, screamed, and tried to convince you to stay married. They may have even told you that they hate you. Rest assured, you are still their parent and like every other child that has ever existed, they still need their parents. Carve out time in your week to spend time with them and ONLY them and get that time approved by their other parent. I know it sounds awful, the thought of communicating and asking permission from the one who left you can be quite trying, but it is better that you feel the weight of this responsibility than your child. They didn't cause this divorce, so do not ask them to carry the weight of it.

Therefore, be sensitive to your children. They are having to adjust to a whole new way of living that they didn't choose. They will never be able to have Christmas with their whole family again. Though they may have more Thanksgiving dinners, there will always be a parent missing from the dinner table. At the end of all their sporting events, theatrical productions, and awards days, they will have to decide which parent to approach first. Divorce is hard for children, and it never really gets better for them. Over time, they can adjust to their new way of life, but they will still forever bear the brunt of their parents divorce more so than either of their parents. Encourage your children to go to whichever parent they want at events in which both parents are present. Make sure they know that you love them and that you will not be the least bit disappointed if they choose to spend time with their other parent over you. Their actions may really hurt you, but your children don't need to know that.

Make no mistake, I am asking you to love your children in a sacrificial way that is very challenging—more so than parents who have remained married will ever know. Therefore, it is critical that you surround yourself with a great group of people to help support and encourage you in this. Seek out friends. Seek out family. Seek out a community that will desire the best for you. One of the best places I have learned to find such community is within a good church. For most churches, it is their desire to help their attendees make the wisest decisions possible for their lives and for their families. Churches have amazing support groups and counseling available, and it's usually free. I work at a church, and I am thrilled to counsel people who are struggling. I take no delight in their struggle, but I hope I can help. By no means am I or any other church employee a miracle worker, but often allowing someone else with an unbiased opinion to listen to the current realities of your life with freedom to speak truthfully can yield incredibly good results.

What your children need

Your children need to become your top priority on earth, and this priority cannot be purchased with money but only with time and compassion. Your child's world has been turned upside down. They have either had to move or have seen a parent move out of the house. I guarantee you that life is not going the way they wish it would. I do not say this to hurt your feelings or to judge you but instead to give you their current reality so that you can care for them during this incredibly difficult time. Here are 5 things you can do to help them in this transition.

1. Make it very clear to them that, though things didn't work out with their parents' marriage, you will never leave them in a million years. They need to understand that just because your union with their mother or father has ended, you will never stop being their parent or that you will never stop spending time around them. They need to know that there is no bigger fan than you in the stands cheering them on and that you'll always be there.

2. Give them a say in where they spend their time. This is going to be really hard because the temptation that most parents face is to try to make their house and time with their children better than the other parent's, and that often results in spoiling a child. Do not attempt to bribe your children so that they will want to spend time with you. Instead, spend quality time with them, have fun with them, but set wise boundaries and don't give in to their every demand. Tell them over and over again that you love them and those boundaries are there because you love them. Children need and long for stable loving relationships more than they need toys, even if they can't always express this.

3. Never speak harshly about their other parent. Remember, that is still your child's mother or father. Your children do not need to hear you criticize their other parent—even if they are deserving of it. Your spouse may act like the incarnation of Satan

himself, but they are still the parent of your child and therefore deserving of your child's respect. If you do not model that respect, then it is very possible that your child will fail to learn or practice respect for either parent. There is no scenario where your children respect their parents if the parents don't respect one another.

4. When you attend events in your child's life, whether it be a basketball game, school awards day, or their wedding day, be sure to encourage your child to not feel pressured to spend equal time with both parents. These days are intended for them to enjoy and celebrate their successes. Encourage your children to enjoy these kinds of days and not worry about how their parents will get along. The other children whose parents are not divorced do not think twice about which parent they greet first, why should yours have to bear such a burden?

5. Strive to make your home a place where your children are comfortable bringing their friends. This may sound like I'm asking you to spend money on the yard and the carpet, but I promise you, I'm not. I'm asking you to keep your home clean and welcoming. People and children especially feel welcomed when someone greets them when they come over and offers them a snack or invites them to play a game. Make a place in your house, apartment, room, etc. for people to sit down and enjoy a meal and/or a game together. This creates fun moments, good memories, and will help your children to feel

much more comfortable in your home, even though they are missing one of their parents.

Should my kids know who I am dating now?

As a child of divorced parents, I can tell you that it is always best to be open and honest with your children— even about dating. When two people pursue a romantic relationship, it is almost impossible to keep such a thing a secret. It is very likely that your child will learn about your relationship. If they do not learn it from you, they will learn it from others. Is that how you want your children to discover who their parents are dating? Be honest and open with your children about who you're dating. Introduce your date to your children. They will have to meet eventually if your relationship is to continue and thrive. Also, don't be afraid to ask your children what their thoughts are on the person whom you're seeing. Your dating has a direct effect on them, and if they do not like the person, then you may need to consider ending the relationship for your sake. Dates come and go, but your children are a blessing you should never fail to consider.

Your children will need to like the person who you are dating. If they don't, they will dread being in your home when your boyfriend/girlfriend is there, and they will dread learning that he or she is on the way over. However, if your children do enjoy the person you're dating and your relationship were to turn into a marriage, it is very important that you set wise boundaries between your new spouse and your children. Your new spouse will definitely see your children at their best and at their worst. Your child's step-parent, must understand that they are not your child's mother or father. Often, step-parents will try to discipline a child, and it rarely ever works out in a way that is good or beneficial. Children rarely show their step-parents the same degree of respect as they would to their biological parents and care little for their opinion or correction. Children can have a good relationship with a step-parent but it rarely is as meaningful as a relationship with a parent who is actively involved in their life. It is always best for you as their parent to do the correcting and make sure the person you are dating or your spouse knows this and honors your wishes.

CHAPTER 5

Understanding Divorced Parents

Unfortunately many children receive little education on how and why Mom and Dad react and behave differently after having a divorce. They are often left to navigate the emotional bomb that exploded in their life with little help or guidance from their parents who are reeling from their own divorce This chapter is meant to help children better understand their parents in light of divorce.

Though your parents may have recently divorced, know that they still love you! It may be difficult to understand. Your home-life has suddenly changed, and it is disorienting. Through it all, your Mom and Dad still love you.Whether your parents divorced when you were 3 or when you were 30, it can often feel as if they have forgotten about you, your desires, and your comfort. But, they are likely doing what they think is best for them so that they can care for you better. This is rarely ever true, but it is what they believe and I have never seen a child (even an adult child) be able to convince their parents to remain married or to get back together. Therefore my hope for you is that you would simply know that your mom and dad still love you. They may not be showing it very well....but they still do.

Your parents will likely want you to spend time with each of them, which sounds good until you realize that you didn't gain any extra days, hours, or minutes in your week. What used to take two hours to hangout with your parents will now take over four hours. Your parents may not understand that divorce takes a lot of time from their children if they are to spend time with both parents. As a child of divorced parents, you may have to learn to say "no": "No" to overcommitting your time and "No" to trying to enjoy one holiday with two sets of families. Do not feel guilty if you only want to spend the weekend with one parent. That is okay. I know so many who try to spend a half-day with Mom and a half-day with Dad, and at the end of the day they feel exhausted. They were never able to truly sit down and unwind with their family because they had to be somewhere soon and couldn't live in the moment.

Be willing to speak gently and truthfully to your parents. If you only want to spend the weekend with one of them, it does not mean you love the other less, and while they both may want you to spend time with them, they will learn to understand that your love for them isn't based on the amount of time you have with each, but it is the quality of time you have. Divorce has real consequences for everyone involved, including your parents. Sometimes, those consequences mean that they get to spend less time with you, which is okay. Consequences teach us and can make us better people. Choosing to get a divorce often means choosing to see your children less and your parents need to understand that and unfortunately you, their child, may be the one who has to tell them. When you convey this truth it may result in some hurt feelings, tears, and perhaps anger. It is much better for you to convey this truth now rather than spend week after week and month after month sacrificing your time and friends just so you can accommodate your parents' divorce.

It never ends

In time, your parents will likely both heal significantly from their divorce. For a while, it will be awkward for them to see one another in public or at your events. They will learn to become civil with one another, especially as they move on with future relationships. Yet, the same cannot be said for you, their child. Your parents divorce will always be a factor in your life. You will always have to split time, days, and holidays between them. You will have to explain to your friends how your two families (that used to be one) are different, and if you date/marry someone you, will have to introduce and guide them through your split family, including your future children. Some of the effects will be more immediate. You will likely have to move or help one of your parents move. You may even have to take on new step-siblings, half-siblings, and have to decide what is to be done with a family pet. The challenges brought on by divorce never end for the children of divorce. It's important to be aware of these things.

Your parents may have thought divorce is something that could allow you to have a better life without arguing. However, it is not uncommon for divorce to come with its own unique challenges. They may say that you will not have to hear them argue again and that you can do more fun things together. While some of that may be true very rarely do children ever view their parents' divorce as something to be grateful for. Most parents want their children to be happy and enjoy life, and that is what they are trying to accomplish for you when they attempt to build up post-divorce life. Though this next part of your life will come with its own challenges, your parents have good intentions in their heart, which is a good place to start. When they tell you that you will be happier with them no longer being together they are most likely wrong but their intention is to make your life as good and as enjoyable as possible because they love you and they want to love you well, they just don't alway know how to do that.

Future Dating

Eventually, your parents will most likely begin dating someone else. This can be a very weird thing to experience as their child. No one can ever replace your mother and father, and that includes the person they date. Consequently, the person they date should only try to be a friend to you. They can be a friend who offers wisdom and counsel from their years of life experience, but they cannot replace your mother or father. If they do try to claim authority over you that they do not rightfully have, or if you notice them having any kind of a negative impact on your parent, it is your duty and responsibility to let your parents know how you feel. I earnestly hope your parents will take your opinion into account when they make decisions about who they will date and romantically pursue, but if they don't you must share how you feel. This will give your parents a chance to love you well.

Approach the subject gently. Often, when our parents get a divorce they feel very lonely and greatly desire to be known and loved again. This desire can lead them to make some unwise decisions about who they date out of fear that they won't have many opportunities for dating and marriage due to their age and stage of life. But, they need to know if they are dating someone who is not treating you well. A divorced parent's dating decisions should always be rooted in the questions of whether or not the person they are dating is good for their child. Essential elements of their decision making should be about you and whether or not the person whom they are dating respects your relationship with both of your parents. If they try to independently parent that child or if they are negligent when they are with them then you must make your mom or dad aware of this issue. Do this with an honest and yet truthful tone and spirit.

CHAPTER 6

Lost Family time

Divorce always leads to a decrease in time spent with your family. When your parents live in different homes, you will never be able to spend Christmas with both of them again. You will never have a Thanksgiving dinner together again. Family vacations will become a thing of the past. Though this may be disheartening, I write this to prepare you for post-divorce life. You will still be able to have wonderful memories and memorable holidays, birthdays, and vacations, but life will never be like it was before. You will often feel tension as both of your parents may want you to spend holidays with them or expect you to split holidays in half between the two of them. When your parents expect you to overexert yourself to accommodate both of them, they are in a sense asking you to pay for their divorce. If they had not divorced, you could spend time with them together and have more free time for yourself and friends. So, if you get tired of going back and forth between them sit down with them and tell them lovingly and gently that you don't enjoy having to go back and forth as a result of their divorce.

Remarriage & Parents

It is likely that one, if not both, of your parents will remarry. I realize that may be weird, awkward, and frustrating to consider, but it's true. A family with a step-parent will have its own unique tensions, but that does not give you the right to be inconsiderate or dismissive to your step-parents. Treat your step-parents with as much respect and care as you can. Though, I do not believe it is wise for step-parents to assume the role of father or mother to their step-children. It is best if they simply try to be a friend and when their step-children misbehave (as all children do) to discipline them by reminding that their mother or father will find out what they have been doing if they do not stop (Of course if any child is about to engage in an activity that could physically harm them without their parents consent then do intervene and stop it.)

Parents, it would be incredibly wise for you to prepare yourself to see your children less if you have chosen to get a divorce. I hope for your child's sake that, when the dust settles from your divorce, they have two parents who desire to love and care for them well. If that is to be the case, then you must encourage your child to spend time with their other parent——no matter how hurt or disappointed you are with them (assuming the other parent does not physically abuse your child). Children need both their mother and father to help them to grow up to be emotionally and mentally healthy. If it takes a man and a woman to make a child, then it seems logical that it would take a mother and a father to raise a child. Moms, no matter how much you love your sons, you cannot teach them how to be good men who know how to lead and love others without being bullies or passive. Dads, no matter how much you love your daughters, you cannot teach them how to be wise women who know how to handle the pressures that society puts on them. Sons also need nurturing from their mothers, and daughters need to feel safe and secure in the arms of their fathers. Parents, encourage your children to spend time with your ex.

If your child plays sports, performs in plays, or displays their artwork, I highly encourage you to go to their events and cheer for them with all you have. However, when their event ends be sure to give them the freedom to go with whichever parent they want. For children with divorced parents, the most tense part of any performance is not on the stage, court, or field, it's in the audience after the event is over. Should they go hug Mom or Dad? Who should they disappoint today? Be sure to tell your child that you love them no matter who they choose first and that you will never be disappointed with them over who they go to first (You may in all reality be disappointed when your child runs to their other parent, but that is between you and your ex not you and your child ...therefore do not let your child ever see your disappointment.)

If your former spouse still wants to spend time with your child, then there is no way to avoid seeing your children less after a divorce. It is important to understand that our source of joy and contentment cannot come from our family or children. I love my wife and sons with all my heart, but they are not where my hope & joy is found. If they were, that would mean that I hated my life when I was single, but I didn't. I was content then just as I am now. Do not bank all of your hope and joy on your children loving you and thinking that you are the best parent ever. Instead, focus your energy on how you can be as lovingly considerate to your child as possible. One day, your child will grow up and leave the nest, but they will come back for many visits if they believe you put their interests ahead of your own.

CHAPTER 7

Lost Finances

If you are currently married and considering getting a divorce, let me encourage you to strongly reconsider. If nothing else, you're about to lose a whole bunch of money. I have never seen a divorce that did not financially scar both parties. The financial effects of a divorce last long after you list your assets and fight over who gets the car, the house, and alimony. A divorce takes all the hard work that you and your spouse have done to save money and make a living for yourself and destroys it--not only for yourselves but your children as well. According to thebalance.com "Arguably the most devastating cost of divorce is its effect on the family, but divorce can also be financially damaging. Your income may be affected, and it's possible that you could find yourself leaving the marriage with high debt." So, if there is any hope of saving your marriage and preventing the monumental amount of financial strain that a divorce will bring on your life, do it! But if not, then this chapter is for you.

In every divorce, you will lose money. It may be money now or money you could have had in the future had you and your spouse avoided a divorce. When couples build a life together, they build it on their combined incomes, talents, and resources. When they divorce, they each have to let half of that go, but they still have the expectation of having their wants fully met. That's why so many lose or gain massive amounts of weight because their daily rhythm of life has been violently disrupted and it will never be the same again.

For a period of time, my wife and I used to live near Louisville, KY. Louisville is known for having very wealthy districts and subdivisions. Many of these families acquired their wealth over several generations. Typically, someone in their family worked hard, stewarded their money well, and when they died, they were able to pass on a generous amount to their children. Those children likewise worked hard and were able to add to their family's wealth and pass on an even greater amount of wealth to their children. As wealth accumulated from one generation to the next, the family was able to make greater investments and in times of prosperity achieve a much greater return that would allow them to survive times of poverty and recession. However, this was only made possible by maintaining marriages and preventing divorce. In a divorce, everything is split--including the inheritance of children.

Often, when a mother or father is desiring to set aside funds for their child to use should the parents face an untimely end, they will leave the funds to be overseen by their spouse or a trusted relative. There are some severe legal ramifications for leaving an inheritance to a person under the age of 18, not to mention how often are teenagers wise with how they spend money? I know I certainly wasn't at that age. Therefore by leaving an inheritance to a spouse (the child's other parent) you can rest easy knowing that if you were to die your spouse can oversee the funds and spend them wisely for your child until they are mature enough to handle such responsibility. But in the event of a divorce your spouse is sometimes legally able to take those funds for themselves. They can easily claim that those funds are in their name and they need them to maintain the lifestyle that they have grown accustomed, and as a result, the money that you intended to leave for your children, to help pay for their education, or perhaps for a future down payment on a house is gone. It might be hard to imagine how someone could ever do that to their child, but this happens quite often.

Many divorced couples are forced to sell their homes because neither of them can afford to pay the mortgage and manage the upkeep of the property on their own. This forces divorced couples to work together (something they have proven to be bad at), to find a realtor, prepare the house for showings, and negotiate a selling price and deal. If two people can no longer stand to live together, then they have little chance whatsoever of peacefully negotiating the sale of a major piece of property. Even if they are able to prepare, manage, and sell a major piece of property, they both have to deal with the fact that they can't enjoy the full profit that they made on the sale. They now have to split the profits and so all the time and effort they spent earning money to pay off the mortgage will only come back to them half fold. Investors will tell you that that is one of the worst returns you can ever receive. Divorce cripples people financially and the effects can last for decades.

Not only do couples lose money on the sale of property, but they also have to incur the additional costs of moving their belongings, finding a new place to live, and perhaps even renting out a storage unit until they can afford a new place to live that can house all of their belongings. The monthly expenditure of child support that most men are required to pay to help provide for their children every month until their children reach 18 years of age is also a significant financial impact. There are two things about child support that cause people deep emotional pain: For the one who is paying, they have no control over how the other parent spends that money. Money that is given to be spent on food, clothing, and shelter for their children can be spent frivolously, and there's nothing the payer can do about it. As for the one receiving the child support, there is the regular frustration of acquiring the funds and hoping their former spouse will pay because it is a long process to legally make someone pay their child support.

While this chapter may have seemed like a rehashing of your own financial nightmare if you have been divorced, I have provided it as a warning to the still-married. No one person can truly complete another, but breaking a marital commitment can financially rip a person apart. Stay married. If it's too late for you, there is still reason for hope. That hope is found in forgiveness of both your former spouse and yourself since a divorce is usually the fault of both spouses. The financial pitfalls of a divorce are absolutely brutal, but they are not absolute. They can be recovered from and financial stability can be reached after a divorce. Yet, there is another devastating dimension to a divorce.

The emotional burden of a divorce is often astronomically greater than the financial one.

Let me encourage you to not let your divorce make you cynical. The world is not out to get you. God has not singled you out to make you suffer. I don't doubt that if we look at how you began your previous marriage, we can easily find some unwise decisions that you made, which led you into a toxic relationship. If we looked at how you chose to handle your frustrations with your former spouse, we would realize that there were healthier ways of handling them. What this means is that there is incredible hope for you. If your decisions helped to lead to your divorce, then that means that if you make different decisions in the future then you could enjoy a wonderful marriage with more financial stability in your life.

CHAPTER 8

❖

God's Perspective (Even in Divorce, There is Hope)

I have often heard that it is best to deliver bad news first when there is good news as well. So here is the bad, but true news first: "If he hates and divorces his wife," says the Lord God of Israel, "he covers his garment with injustice" (Malachi 2:16). It's true, the God of the universe hates the fact that you, your friends, your parents, and your children have to experience divorce. He likens it to when someone commits murder--they usually have the stain of blood on themselves. Divorce doesn't stain us with blood, but it does stain us with broken relationships and severed relational connections that will never heal. It is not God's hope or desire for your life. But, God is still the source of hope and joy in the world, not to mention the ultimate expression of love. It is important to know that your divorce does not have to be what defines you. Your failed marriage is not meant to doom your future if you allow God to guide you. God is in the business of restoring people all over the world from every nation, and He would like nothing more than to restore you and your life from the pits of despair, sadness, and loneliness. That's the good news.

Jesus, who was God in the flesh, was questioned about divorce multiple times. Why? Some people then, just like people now, were not sure what to do when they were in a marriage that they were no longer enjoying. Others had already attained a divorce because they thought it would improve their lives; they soon realized that every divorce comes with baggage and they were wondering if they had made the right decision. When asked, Jesus told them this, "Have you not read that he who created them from the beginning made them male and female, and said, 'Therefore a man shall leave his father and his mother and hold fast to his wife, and the two shall become one flesh'? So they are no longer two but one flesh. What therefore God has joined together, let not man separate." (Matthew 19:4-6) The imagery in Jesus's words suggests that divorce is like mutilation. Tearing apart one flesh. It is not God's desire for anyone to experience the heartbreak of a divorce for a wide variety of reasons. All of the negative effects of divorce that have been mentioned in this book add validity to that. But there is still hope for you and your life ahead. Checkout the following story of Jesus providing in a situation that seemed completely void of it.

When Jesus was crucified on the cross there were two convicted criminals on each side of him. They each had very different perspectives on being publicly executed next to Jesus as they voiced their opinions.

³⁹ Then one of the criminals hanging there began to yell insults at Him: "Aren't You the Messiah? Save Yourself and us!"

⁴⁰ But the other answered, rebuking him: "Don't you even fear God, since you are undergoing the same punishment? **41** We are punished justly, because we're getting back what we deserve for the things we did, but this man has done nothing wrong." **42** Then he said, "Jesus, remember me when You come into Your kingdom!"

⁴³ And He said to him, "I assure you: Today you will be with Me in paradise." (Luke 23:39-43)

Whenever we experience bad things in life, be it our own fault or the fault of others we have two options: (1) to get mad at the world including God OR (2) to accept that what has happened to us is real and that complaining will not fix it and that we must respond wisely to it. It is God's desire for us to seek out good community for both ourselves and our children whether we are single, married, divorced, or widowed. We are meant to be born in community with our mother and father, we are meant to grow up in community with our friends and siblings, and we are meant to pursue good friendships and relationships well into our adult years. The criminal on the cross sought out a relationship with Jesus...and you can too on both a personal and communal level. If you invite Jesus into your life to be your Lord and Savior He will most assuredly save you and never leave you.

From pursuing Godly community you can find a new person to romantically pursue who is also trying to be the person God wants them to be who is desiring to love others truly as they love themselves. You can join forces in honoring Jesus with your lives, and you can learn from the mistakes of your previous marriage. You can have a wonderful marriage in the future. The criminal on the cross next to Jesus did not see a positive future for himself. You can understand why....he was on a cross sentenced to die for a crime he committed. But Jesus promised him something else for his future. Because of his faith in Jesus, he got to spend the day and eternity to follow in paradise (Heaven) with Jesus. Because of your faith and obedience to Jesus you too can find a person with the same faith for a bright marriage in your future.

But I do want to caution you in trying to find someone to remarry. Remember that a new spouse cannot make your life better, Jesus is our only source of joy in this life. Also the Bible has some important instruction about when it is wise and unwise to remarry. In the case of a marriage ending due to adultery or abandonment the Bible states that you are no longer bound to that person (Matthew 5:32 & 1 Corinthians 7:10-16) and in many cases are free to remarry. But I would encourage you to reach out to a faithful pastor at a local church to inquire about the Bible and how it relates to your divorce. If you don't know a local pastor, feel free to reach out to me. I would love to try to help you. My email is in the next chapter.

Your children still love you

There is no doubt that your divorce will affect your children for the rest of their life. It is never easy for children to experience the separation of their mother and father. Their lives will never be the same. That said, they can in time forgive you and they do still love you. No one else will ever be their mother or father and they know that. From a young age children know who Mom and Dad are...and they don't forget it. Yet, the questions of 'why', 'what', and 'how' may still remain with your child. It's important for your children to be able to make sense of why you got a divorce, what caused it, and what you can teach them from it. Far too often, parents want to try to sweep it under the rug in an attempt to conceal their child from the awful things that lead to a divorce (adultery, abuse, neglect etc.) but in time when your children are at an appropriate age, if they want to know what caused your divorce sit down with them and love them enough to tell them the truth. Who knows? Perhaps after hearing your story they will have the knowledge to make wiser choices in the future for their spouse and for your grandchildren.

If you decide to take what you've learned from your previous marriage: the ways your former spouse fell short and the ways you fell short (there are no perfect people in this world), and you want to attempt to date and potentially marry someone else, then include your children in the process. A new step-parent will not fix the emotional damage that a divorce brings on children (whether they are still minors or adults), but opening lines of communication about your dating decisions will be greatly appreciated by them. Whoever you choose to spend time with as a parent will have a direct effect on your children. Children don't get to have a say in who their biological parents are, they don't get to have a say in whether or not their biological parents will stay together, therefore shouldn't they get to have a say in who their potential step-parents are? Children suffer the most in a divorce, let's not ask them to suffer more by making them share a home with someone they may not like, trust, or with whom they feel safe.

CHAPTER 9

I wrote this book because I encountered many challenges as a child that not many of my friends did because the majority of their parents never divorced. However, as I grew older into my young adult years, I began to notice that many in the graduating classes coming up after me were experiencing the same challenges that I did: divorced parents. One person in particular who I noticed was the woman who would become my wife. Her parents divorced during her senior year of college, shortly before we started dating. I noticed that there were few resources out there to help her cope with the impending reality that her life would never be the same. That Christmas', Thanksgivings, and Birthdays are never going to look the same. The major milestones in her life were now going to include tension over whether or not her parents could stand to sit next to one another at her college graduation, our wedding day, or at our son's first birthday. These challenges aren't unique to my wife's parents, they're common to all children of divorce. So this book has been written to help the children of those parents, divorced parents, and their friends around them.

I hope this book has and will continue to be an aid to you and your situation. But please know that I am here for you as well (mackey.gaskin@gmail.com). Do not hesitate to email me.

My mom and dad divorced when I was very young. I have no memory of our little family of three doing anything together. It was very challenging for me to go back and forth between them on my own. But, my parents loved me fiercely and they never stopped working at their friendship with one another and they eventually were able to become friendly enough to talk politely about one another and in time they were able to speak cordially and friendly with one another. No matter how bad your divorce was, your children need you to be friends again. A little peace between you and your child's other parent will bring a world of security to your children.

I genuinely love my parents. The reason I love them today is because they never quit working to provide more peace in my life. They continually kept working through their anger, frustration, and disappointment with one another to love me better and better. As a young child I remember them arguing whenever one would drop me off with the other. As an adult, I remember them helping me to get ready for college, preparing for my first job in my career, and even helping to prepare and clean up the decorations for my wedding. My childhood may not have been ideal, but my years of adulthood are going very well. In time, your children's forgiveness and love for you can grow. Do not ask them to pay for your divorce by pressuring them to spend time with you instead of your ex and learn to forgive your ex and you'll most likely find that your children will forgive you as well. The bond between children and a parent is not easily broken.

Now as an adult with children of my own, I'm grateful for the time and effort my parents spent talking about me, because raising a child is HARD. It is not God's desire for any of us to live life solely on our own let alone raise a child on our own. Therefore, even if you do not agree with the other parent's style, you still need to make contact with them just to learn how your child's day was at school or if they are behaving differently in any way. Your child may not like it, but they are not the boss and they are not capable of raising themselves alone. Talk to their other parent, for the sake of your child.

Never Walk Alone

You were not meant to raise children on your own. Even if your ex wants nothing to do with you or your child you still were not meant to raise a child on your own. I'm not saying you can't do it, many have, but it is not God's desire for life to be that challenging for you, which is why he provided the local church. I cannot stress to you how important it is for you to go to a local church consistently. It's a great way to learn more about God and the wisdom of the Bible, but it's also a great place to find community. You'll be able to talk with other parents who are in a similar season of life and great friendships will be developed in your life. Your child will also have the opportunity to make friendships in a wonderful environment where other well trained faithful adults can serve as mentors to them and aid you in raising your child. You'll be able to meet older parents who can share their wisdom with you and answer any questions you have about raising a little one. No church is perfect or will ever be perfect because no single person other than Jesus is perfect. Therefore there are plenty of ways that churches and church member can disappoint you, and you them, but if you are willing to come together with a group who is willing to admit that they need Jesus and one another to better follow Jesus you'll find that raising your child in God's community is way better than going at it alone.

While attending a weekly church service can be a wonderful experience, you'll find that you make your closest friendships and connections in a small group Bible study. I used to be afraid of these groups because I didn't know much about what the Bible said, but let me tell you a little secret: The Bible is HUGE!!!! Few church members know it cover to cover which is why church groups break down into smaller groups to study the Bible and to develop wonderful communities with one another. Your kids will also benefit greatly from being in a youth group with a faithful leader. If you've been a parent for long you know that in time your kids can drown your voice out. They hear it often & just like us they grow tired of hearing the same repetitive sounds and words over & over. But when a kind youth leader speaks to your child and gets to know them...it can change their life. Their youth leader can say the same exact thing to them that you are...but with a different voice from a different perspective and your kids just might take it to heart. We all need someone who we can talk to who cannot threaten us with punishment. That's what a good youth leader can be to your child.

Not to mention the social skills your children will pick up and grow as a result of a youth group. Teachers and therapists all over the United States are reporting that more and more of their students and pediatric patients are suffering from a lack of social skills and friendships. In Church, children are encouraged to set aside their phone and pick up a friend. In Bible studies, children can put Snapchat away and hear directly from the God who created them. He knows them so much better than their social media, or their classmates, or even you do as their parent. Children can flourish in so many wonderful and beautiful ways when they get to have face to face time with others kids, learn about God, and have wise & caring mentors who pour into them and you can find all of this in a good local church that is striving to be faithful to God and the Bible.